THE MISSING SOUL

THE MISSING SOUL

FILIP KUJAWA

This is a biographical novel; I have written this to try and let go of my trauma. Some sections of this novel are true, while the rest is just made up. However, everything written in these pages are things that have happened or things that I have imagined.

This book is dedicated to everyone that is struggling or wanting to understand the struggles of people.

All the best,
Filip.

CONTENTS

Chapter 1
Never Ending Trauma

My palms are sweaty, my leg bouncing and my body shaking. The clock ticks, anticipation builds up. I rest my head on my desk, hoping that time will miraculously speed up. Although something feels off, I lift my head up and there's my teacher, looking straight at me shooting me an annoyed look. Suddenly, all eyes are on me, and I can't help to wonder if I messed up again.

Reality snaps back when the teacher speaks up, giving the class the sign to leave. The walk of shame it is, I think to myself. I get up from my seat but just as I come to open the door she calls my name, "Filip". My heart skips a beat as I turn to face her. "Can you please stay back a second" she says to me.

She waits for everyone to leave before asking me to sit down in front of her. Anxiety starts to consume me, and I can't help but feel overwhelmed by what she wants to talk about.

She begins to tell me that I need to start paying more attention in class and especially to stop falling asleep otherwise I will fail my exams. I tilt my head down knowing she's right. She begins to ask me why I fall asleep so much in her lesson, I'm at a loss of words and so I shrug.

I leave in a hurry; I couldn't stand being in that classroom any longer. I walk out of the gates and notice my friends have left me to walk home alone. I start walking, feeling anxious that anyone from school could approach me and hurt me, anything can happen. I manage to catch up to my friend Darcy but then someone else manages to catch up to me, someone I couldn't recognise.

They had a puffy coat with their hood up and a balaclava covering their face except the eyes. "Filip, you better watch out as it's not going to end well for you. I've seen the stuff you have been posting on social media about me, about everybody." They turn around and walk away.

Darcy looks at me in shock. I tell her that I have no idea what he was going on about and so she gets her phone to check social media. She searches my name up and my account is there, but the one below has the same username and profile picture.

Whilst still walking I take her phone and go onto the account. Hundreds of posts about what everyone seems to think is me, commenting about various people in the school, discriminating them all. Who would do this?

I enter my house and get changed out of my school uniform. I eat some food and crawl into bed. I feel drained, to the point where I end up sleeping away to escape reality. Why would someone make a fake account of me? As I begin to drift away, I get a call from Darcy. I pick up and they ask if I can hang out with them. All I want to do is sleep but Darcy continues to speak.

They say that we should hang out instead of me sleeping all the time. I figure I should focus my mind on something positive instead of being lost in an endless loop of thoughts and so I agree and get ready.

Some half an hour later I arrive at the local town where I used to go often, Radtion. This is where we decided to meet up. I hoped they'd be here before me but as usual, Darcy is running late. As time is passing, I walk into a shop to get a drink. Darcy is calling again. "Hey Filip, I'm just outside the shop waiting for you now". I hang up and walk over to them.

The first thing I ask is who that guy was after school, and they respond saying that they have no idea. We head over to a restaurant and order some food. They start talking to me about a friend of ours and ask whether she is ok or not. I say that I haven't heard from her in a while as we aren't really close friends anymore.

Darcy mentions that they are worried about her as she hasn't been turning up to school recently. I reassure Darcy, telling them that she is probably dealing with her own issues at the moment and that once Taylor figures them out, she'll return to school.

We pay and start heading home, Darcy mentions a funny inside joke to me to which we both start laughing hysterically. They stopped laughing and pulled me aside. "Look who it is" they say to me in a whisper. I turn and pick up the pace whilst dragging Darcy along.

It was a group of people from our school, some of which had already finished school in the previous years. The group start to follow us. We walk around Radtion but they catch up. "Do you think it was one of them?" Darcy says to me. I shrug whilst thinking that it probably is one of them. They bully me a lot in school, getting everyone to hate me. I never know why though.

Every time I take a step, I can feel their presence lurking behind me. I can't shake the feeling that danger was closing in, I feel like a helpless pawn in this twisted place. I run through an old black arched door which led to a dark alleyway with Darcy, I shut the door behind me, then I lock it.

Sweat rushes through my body, fear does too. Every step I had taken seemed to lead me deeper into the darkness. The fear wraps around me like a suffocating fog, making it tricky to breathe.

Oscar bangs on the door, I feel like I'm standing on the edge between safety and imminent danger. His mates shout and say that if we don't open up, they will break down the door. In this moment I am breaking down, I am afraid of what they want from me. Darcy suggests opening the door and talking to them, but I beg Darcy not to open it.

I am terrified of the endless possibilities of what will happen when that door is opened. I plead them not to open it. Darcy starts talking to Oscar. Darcy asks that if we open the door, can we have a civilised conversation. I plead them not to open it once again, but they do anyway once Oscar agrees.

Seven guys walk in including Oscar, wearing balaclavas and puffy coats making them look a lot bigger than they are. "What do you want Oscar?" I question him in a shaken voice. He tells me to shut up and get on my knees to apologise. In this moment I feel a lack of control, I couldn't get out of this situation.

Not in school, not at home and not even in Radtion, anywhere a situation occurs I can't escape it, having to deal with the pain no matter what. I was unsure of what he meant by apologise, I have not done anything to him, the only times we've interacted was when he had something horrible to say about me.

I don't know what I was supposed to apologise for and if anything, shouldn't it be him to apologise for making me feel helpless and embarrassed wherever I go. One of his mates is telling Oscar to fight me. He moves closer to me, I move back. Oscar lunges at me with force.

His arm tightens around me, squeezing my throat, but I refuse to surrender. I tilt my head down, denying him the satisfaction of choking me. The sound of their laughter fills the air as his mates eagerly capture the assault on their phones. Darcy, the one I thought was my friend, abandons me to face this brutality alone.

With a forceful shove, Oscar propels me into a wall, my head colliding with a resounding crash. Pain shoots through me, and I feel warm blood trickling down my face, but I summon every ounce of strength to push back. Anger and indignation surge within me, a burning desire for justice, for him to pay for his actions. But before I can retaliate, I find myself overwhelmed, outnumbered. He hurls me to the ground, and darkness engulfs my senses as consciousness slips away.

I wake up, my head pounding with pain. Each throb feels like a hammer against my skull, making it hard to think straight. The sun has set, and I check my phone, it's 10:32 PM. Slowly, I manage to stand up, feeling dizzy and disoriented. The world around me appears hazy, as if I'm viewing it through a foggy lens.

I stumble out of the alleyway, only to find it empty, with no sign of Darcy. Covered in warm blood and tears streaming down my face, I clean myself up with tissues from my pockets, my hands feeling numb. As I enter my house, I climb upstairs and cry myself to sleep, the pain and loneliness weighing heavily on my heart.

I wake up, feeling the heat engulfing me, my joggers rolled up to my knees. I grab my phone, the time glaring at me, 4:12 AM. A dozen unread messages from Darcy await, but I choose to ignore them, craving a few more hours of sleep. My mind however refuses to rest, battling with pain. As I rise, my head starts pounding, but I push through, tiptoeing downstairs to avoid waking anyone.

I grab a drink with the thought of school looming over me. The fear of being ridiculed, of the video being seen by everyone, weighs heavy. Just then, my phone buzzes, adding to the turmoil.

Chapter 2
Plan & Escape

1 New message from Taylor:
Hey Filip, are you awake??

Why would she message me? I decide to open the message and reply to her.

Me: Hey are you ok?

Taylor: No not really, I can't sleep at all.

Me: Oh, I'm sorry is something bothering you?

Taylor: Well, kind of. I've been thinking of running away for the past couple of weeks and I feel like I should do it.

I think about what she has just texted me.

Taylor: Hello?

Me: Hey sorry I just thought about what you said.

Taylor: About me running away?

Me: Yeh, I've thought about doing it before, but I'd be scared of what people would say.

Taylor: I would feel scared to but what if we ran away together? Maybe that wouldn't be such a bad idea.

Me: We should do it.

Taylor: Really? Ok. Pack a bag with some clothes and other essentials and meet at Parkes Bay for 5:00 AM

I process the conversation whilst still being traumatised by last night's experience. Running away would be impossible as we'd be found straight away if someone noticed that we went missing, but it couldn't hurt trying.

The weight of everything that's been going on is suffocating me, and I can't handle it anymore. I would finally be away from all this pain. I feel the burning desire to escape, to leave everything behind and start fresh. The thought of running away fills me with a mix of excitement and apprehension.

It's like a rollercoaster of emotions, but deep down, I know it's what I need to do to find myself again. I can't help but wonder what lies ahead, but one thing's for sure: I'm ready to chase for a new beginning, no matter how uncertain it may be.

I get my school bag and empty it, I grab a handful of clothes, I get my toothbrush and some money I have saved up. As I pack, I feel paranoid that I will get caught but also a rush of adrenaline as this escape can lead to a better life.

I open the door slightly; my body starts shaking. I continue to open the door whilst it makes a screeching sound. I leave my house, shut the door and walk without looking back.

As I reach Parkes Bay, I see a figure in the distance of the field standing next to some trees. It waves at me. That must be Taylor. I start walking up to her whilst not being able to see much.

I still find it weird how she messaged me out of the blue, I mean we barely spoke to each other although we are in the same friend group, we'd both just talk to Darcy as she was the most supportive and outgoing in the group, well so I thought. I was furious with them for leaving me last night. But why did Taylor ask me to run away with her?

We start talking and I ask her if she has a plan, she reaches for her bag and pulls out a piece of paper. She points at it saying that it was the plan on how to go missing, first we have to catch a train and then we need to make some money when we reach our destination.

She also mentions how we must change the way we look encase someone was to find or notice us. I notice she's a bit cold and I offer her my jacket. She takes it, says thank you and continues to speak, telling me that we have to head to the train station now as there will be a train leaving at 6:25 AM.

We start to walk through the field, not being able to see what's in front of us. Soon after we see a pathway and some streetlights, from there we make our way to the station. Taylor walks up to the ticket machine and buys two tickets; she passes me one and I look at the destination...

"LONDON!" I yell in disbelief. "Yes, we need to get as far away as possible and no one will find us in

London, it's a massive city." Taylor says to me. I look up to the sky and notice the shade of it is getting lighter. The sun was going to rise soon so we made our way in a hurry and boarded the train.

There are many people here wearing suits whilst holding briefcases, they were probably heading off to work. We took our seats in carriage 8 and waited for the train to leave.

"This train is ready to board, please make sure you have boarded the correct train. This train is heading to London Kings Cross Station and is estimated to arrive at 8:55 AM." The conductor made the announcement and the train started to move. I became very nervous and began to contemplate whether this was a mistake.

Taylor noticed I was at unease and grabbed my hand. She said that it was going to be ok in a calm manner. I felt reassured now and decided to sort out my bag.

I went through everything I brought starting off with my clothes. I folded them so there would more space in the bag and then I went through my wallet to check that I had everything. I had my ID, a photo of my mum and my money. Taylor glanced and asked how much I had. I replied and said that I had £100 to which she said that she had £248 left after buying the tickets. I asked if she wanted me to pay her back for the ticket and she said that it wasn't necessary as we'd have to add up our money anyway to survive.

I keep thinking about what we're doing. I try to make sense of reality. "What do we do when we get there?" I asked in an agitated tone. "We'll have to figure out a place to stay and then look for jobs" she replied with an eager smile.

Taylor looked happy to run away, I mean I am happy too, but the sense of unease just makes me feel like something will go wrong. Like we'll get caught and taken back to live our normal lives.

The train suddenly comes to a stop and the lights go out. Everyone around us begins talking to one another, asking what's going on and why the train has stopped.

The conductor starts to speak "I am sorry to inform that if you are in carriage 6, 7, 8, 9 or 10, you will have to exit the train at this stop. This train will now reach London Kings Cross at approximately 9:03 AM. We apologise for the inconvenience". We look at each other dismayed about the situation and get up to exit the train.

"Where even are we Filip?" Taylor asks, starting to feel unsettled herself. I look around and notice what station we are at. "We are in Stevenage, and it says that the next train will be here in 20 minutes" I reply. I sit down whilst Taylor goes to the vending machine, I feel uncomfortable and perplexed about what I want.

Maybe running away wasn't such a good idea after all, I mean we are bound to get caught once we are declared missing. Taylor comes back and sits down beside me. We talk through our plan a little more in-depth until the train comes, her phone starts ringing, her mum is calling her. Taylor declines, her mum starts messaging her frantically. Taylor switches her phone of as the train is approaching. She rushes up and throws her phone onto the tracks. Is she insane, I hold on to my phone tighter. What on earth did she just do?

We board the train and take our seats to which hopefully we can make it to London without any problems. The train heads off and makes its way, it is currently 7:43 AM. I think about the time, my mum will be up shortly and if she comes into my room and sees I am not there, she'll be half scared to death. She will know immediately that somethings up and if I do not answer the phone, she will be sure to report me as missing as soon as police are involved.

I look at the photo I have of her, even though I believe no one cares about me, I know she does. She will be devastated at the fact that I am missing. I start to tear up a little bit, my nose becomes runny, and my forehead begins to sweat. Tears fall down my cheeks as I think more and more about the reaction my mum will have when I am gone. Maybe I should message her, let her know I'm safe at least. I reach for my phone, and I write out a text to my mum.

Me: Hi mum, when you read this and realise I am not at home, it is because I have decided to leave and start a new beginning for myself. I know there are other options but, in this moment, I feel like there is no other choice. Please know that I love you and that we will see each other soon.

I hesitate for a moment before I send the message, I feel fear in me, guilt in me. I love her so much and I know she will blame herself for my disappearance, she'll think she is a terrible woman, a terrible mother. Taylor rests her head onto my shoulder, I think she's fallen asleep. I switch my phone off and try and have a quick nap before making it to London.

Chapter 3
Reported Missing

The officer picks up the phone and says, "Hello, police speaking." My mum's voice trembles as she speaks frantically, explaining that I wasn't home this morning and she's worried. Suddenly, her phone buzzes with a message from me. As she reads it, tears stream down her face and her breath becomes raspy. She tries her best to speak through her sobs.

The officer kindly tells her to calm down and asks her to explain the situation again. She tells them that I was nowhere to be found when she came to check on me this morning. All she knows is that I ran away instead of being taken, which didn't offer her much relief. The officer advises her to come to the station to file a report and answer some questions before they can start a search.

My mum thanks the police officer and hangs up. As my mum rushes to the police station, her heart pounds in her chest. She can't help but think about all the possible dangers I could be facing. The officer at the station listens attentively to her, assuring her that they will do everything they can to find me. They ask for any additional information that might help in the search.

My mum provides them with a recent photo of me, describing my appearance in detail. She mentions that I was wearing a black hoodie and jeans when she last saw me. The officer takes notes and promises to circulate the information to all the officers in the area. They also inform her that there has been another missing person reported just an hour before with the same story. Me and Taylor were both at home during the evening and then gone before the morning.

Feeling a glimmer of hope, my mum heads back home. She can't bear the emptiness that surrounds her, the silence that echoes through the rooms. She goes into my bedroom, sitting on my bed and clutching my favourite stuffed animal. Tears stream down her face as she imagines me alone and scared out there.

Meanwhile, the search for us intensifies. The police organise teams to comb through the neighbourhood, questioning neighbours and checking local hangouts. Flyers with our photos are distributed, and social media is flooded with posts about our disappearance. The community rallies together, offering support and spreading the word to find us.

We don't want to be found; we want to start fresh where we don't feel like outsiders to the rest of the world. After years of torture at school, people turning everyone against me, I have no other choice but to leave.

I can't live in a place of terror, a place where everyone is out to get me. It had to be Oscar who made that account, just to create a reason to fight me, another reason for people to hate me.

Chapter 4
Start Of A New Life

"We have arrived at London Kings Cross station" the instructor spoke. I turn and notice that Taylor is still asleep, so I shake her lightly, I whisper telling her to wake up. She opens her eyes slowly whilst yawning. I tell her that we've arrived and that we need to get off. We can barely stand up, but we manage to and exit the train station stumbling from side to side, with people looking us up and down.

The news on a nearby screen amplifies our panic as we realise, we're declared missing. It is like a punch to the gut when I see this. I figured we could just run away, escape all the pressure and expectations, but now the whole world knows we're gone.

Panic sets in as I realise the magnitude of what we had done. The weight of the situation crashes down on me, making it hard to breathe. how did things spiral out of control so quickly?

Mixed emotions flood my mind – fear, regret, and a deep sense of unease. I thought we were being bold, taking control of our lives, but now we are lost in a sea of uncertainty.

The thought of my family, especially my mum, worried sick and searching for me, made my heart ache with guilt. I never meant to cause them this pain. But amidst the chaos, a flicker of determination ignites within me. I can't let fear consume me, I have to face the consequences of my actions and find the right path for freedom. Me and Taylor have gone too far, and we can't turn back now.

Taylor quickly finds the nearest thrift shop on my phone to change our appearance, and find a new path to freedom. We hurry there, knowing time is against us. With our hoods up, we step into the shop, hoping to blend in and leave behind any traces of who we used to be.

We rummage through the clothes, finding some nice pieces and others that are a bit worn. We grab a mix of outfits to blend in with the crowd. London's diversity makes it easier to go unnoticed. After paying, we brainstorm ways to further alter our appearance.

Taylor bursts into laughter, keeping the reason a secret. Impatient, I press her for an answer. Finally, she reveals her surprise. We head to a nearby salon where Taylor dyes her hair blonde and adds curls, transforming her look. As for me, Taylor decides I should go all in and get a buzz cut, ensuring I'm unrecognisable. We check ourselves out in the phone camera and surprisingly, we look pretty good. Taylor suggests taking a selfie to capture the moment, and as she looks at me, there's a sense of camaraderie and hope in her eyes.

We stare into each other's eyes while the sun shines at us, her golden curls glow from the sun and a tear falls down her cheek while she smiles. I raise my hand and wipe the tear away. She leans closer to hug me and I hug her back. Time stops for a moment, all I can feel is her warmth and her presence.

This moment feels like a jolt of electricity running through my body, making me feel alive. In this embrace, all my worries and troubles melt away, and I feel this overwhelming sense of comfort.

Taylor feels a sense of security, she whispers into my ear and thanks me for coming with her. I look at her again, like I've known her my whole life, I thank her for suggesting the idea.

We walk looking for a coffee shop nearby, talking about all the things we can do now, the endless possibilities we have in London. I think to myself as we speak that she's not wrong and that the possibilities are practically endless.

We find a coffee shop and we sit next to a window where we can see the Big Ben from a distance. We discuss the next plan, how to make some money. London has thousands of places looking for workers. Taylor suggests we split up and look for places that are hiring and so we pay and leave, then we go our separate ways.

Taylor walks along a bridge, looking over at the water stream and into the horizon. She questions her choices but she's glad she left. Parkes Bay has traumatised her; I don't exactly know what, but I just know it. She didn't come to school often, she was the 'quiet girl', the girl that no one knew existed.

She skipped class a lot and had trouble socialising. All I know is that if we don't get caught, she'll have a better life, a better future, and so will I.

Her eyes catch a glimpse of a designer shop with a vibrant "Now Hiring" sign on the window. Excitement fills her as she steps inside, mustering up the courage to ask the question that could potentially change her life. "Hi there," she says to the sales associate, her voice filled with anticipation. "I noticed the hiring sign. Is the store currently looking for new team members?"

The sales associate nods with a warm smile and directs Taylor towards a young woman named Sophia, who is conducting interviews. As Taylor enters the room, she can't help but feel a tinge of envy. Sophia exudes confidence and poise, her appearance flawless from head to toe. Taylor's nerves intensify as she compares herself to Sophia's seemingly perfect image.

As the interview progresses, Taylor's worries begin to fade. Sophia's demeanour is friendly and welcoming, putting Taylor at ease. They engage in a genuine conversation, discussing Taylor's passion for fashion and her previous retail experience.

Despite her initial jealousy, Taylor finds herself admiring Sophia's professionalism and ability to make her feel comfortable.

To her surprise and delight, Taylor gets offered the job at the designer shop. She feels a surge of pride and accomplishment, knowing that her courage and determination has paid off.

Chapter 5
Survival Begins

As I navigate the streets of the city, my heart beats in sync with the rhythm of my anxious thoughts. The weight of being missing hangs heavy on my shoulders, each step a reminder of the uncertainty that lies ahead.

I find myself drawn to a quaint little shop, its warm glow beckoning me inside. Seeking solace in a simple drink, I push open the door and step into a world that will forever change my path.

The air is thick with anticipation as I approach the counter, ready to place my order. But what I encounter is far from the ordinary. Before me stands an elderly man, the shop's manager, locked in a harrowing struggle with a masked intruder. Time seems to slow as my eyes widen in disbelief. Fear grips my chest, but a surge of adrenaline propels me forward.

In that moment, the world around me fades into the background. Every fibre of my being is focused on protecting the manager, on thwarting the robber's intentions.

I leap onto the intruder. Emotions swirl within me like a tempest, fear intermingled with anger and determination. My heart pounds in my ears, the physical strain of the struggle evident in every muscle of my body.

With each move, I can feel the weight of the situation pressing down upon me. The adrenaline courses through my veins, heightening my senses and sharpening my focus. It's as if time stands still, the room a battleground where bravery and desperation collide.

Finally, after what feels like an eternity, I manage to overpower the intruder. Relief washes over the room, mingled with gratitude and admiration in the manager's eyes.

He approaches me, his voice filled with genuine appreciation, and asks if there's anything he can do to repay me for my bravery. In that moment, an idea takes hold of me, fuelled by a mix of exhaustion and adrenaline.

With a hesitant yet determined voice, I suggest the possibility of working at the shop. The old man's eyes widen, a glimmer of hope shining through his weathered features. He takes a moment to consider, weighing the risks and rewards, before finally nodding in agreement. A sense of gratitude washes over me, knowing that this unexpected turn of events has opened a door to a new opportunity.

As I bid farewell to the manager and step out of the shop, a mix of emotions courses through my veins. Pride swells within me, mingling with a sense of accomplishment and gratitude. The uncertainty that once plagued me now feels like an opportunity, a chance to grow.

So, Taylor and I finally meet up at the London Eye after our job search. We're both bursting with excitement to share our news. Taylor starts gushing about how she absolutely aced her interview, nailing every question with confidence and charm. I can't help but be in awe of her.

Then it's my turn to share my story. I start by saying, "You won't believe what happened to me! I actually stopped a robbery to secure a job!" I go on to describe the intense moment, the adrenaline pumping through my veins as I bravely intervened and saved the day. It's like something out of a movie!

Yet, as twilight descends upon the city, the harsh realities of our predicament cast a somber shadow. We find ourselves bereft of a sanctuary for the night, and the weight of our circumstances begins to gnaw at our spirits. We embark on an odyssey through the labyrinthine streets of London, our voices resonating with a symphony of vexation, trepidation, and vulnerability.

We bare our souls, unburdening ourselves of the traumas that have shaped us. The city becomes our confidante, its bustling rhythm providing a backdrop to our shared catharsis. We may not have a place to call home tonight, but we have each other, and a bench for us to sleep on.

As I slowly drift away my mind focuses on that social media account. That's not the only reason I left, I have been stalked, humiliated and I was attacked.

The urge to run away had crossed my mind a few times, but now that it's a reality, I feel a sense of relief. I can be myself, achieve great things.

Chapter 6
Settling In

As the first rays of dawn break through the city's slumber, Taylor and I stir from our restless sleep on the park benches. Fatigue weighs heavily upon us, yet an undercurrent of excitement courses through our veins, propelling us forward into the unknown. Today marks the beginning of our new lives, our first day of work in this bustling metropolis.

Taylor's eyes shimmer with a blend of anticipation and nervousness as she embarks on her journey to the designer shop. Her passion for fashion is palpable, radiating from her very being. With each step, she exudes a quiet determination, ready to immerse herself in the world of haute couture.

I catch glimpses of her animated conversations with colleagues, her voice infused with a mix of awe and eagerness. The language of style becomes her lexicon, and she effortlessly navigates the intricacies of her new role, leaving an indelible impression on those around her.

As for me, I find myself in a little shop, where the rich aroma of freshly brewed coffee lingers in the air. The melodic chime of the door signals the arrival of customers seeking their morning pick-me-up. With a warm smile and a touch of eloquence, I engage in conversations, guiding them through the myriad of flavours and brewing techniques.

Each interaction becomes a symphony of words, carefully chosen to evoke a sense of delight and curiosity. The language of coffee becomes my muse, and I revel in the art of creating moments of caffeinated bliss for those who grace our humble establishment. This helps me focus on the path that lies ahead of me, and to let go of the past that has been consuming me for years.

In the midst of the bustling city, Taylor and I find solace in our shared experiences. We exchange stories of our encounters, reviling in the language of our respective realms. The vibrancy of the city becomes a backdrop to our conversations, amplifying our emotions and infusing our words with an extra layer of depth. Together, we navigate the labyrinthine streets, our footsteps echoing with a newfound confidence, as we embrace the challenges and triumphs that lie ahead.

And so, with tired yet hopeful hearts, we embark on this remarkable chapter of our lives, ready to embrace the language of our dreams and paint the canvas of our futures with the colours of passion and resilience.

As I walk through the shop Ernest, my manager, catches my attention. He's engaged in a conversation with a customer, their words laced with concern and worry. They speak of two missing teenagers, their disappearance shrouded in mystery. My heart quickens, and a wave of unease washes over me. I can't help but overhear their conversation, my ears straining to catch every word.

Quickly, I concoct an excuse to leave, my mind racing with thoughts of Taylor's safety. I make my way to her workplace, the designer store where she weaves her magic with fabrics and colours. The moment I step inside, I'm greeted by Sophia, a kind-hearted soul who knows Taylor well. I explain the urgency of the situation, my words tumbling out in a rush.

"Taylor, we need to talk. My manager was discussing our disappearance. We can't afford to draw attention to ourselves. We must keep a low profile." I say, my voice filled with urgency and concern. Taylor's eyes widen, mirroring the unease that swirls within me. We exchange glances, aware of the danger that lurks in the shadows.

Together, we huddle in the corner of the store, our voices hushed as we strategise our next move. The language of secrecy becomes our shield, as we carefully choose our words, ensuring they won't raise suspicion. We agree to keep a low profile and I leave, telling Taylor in secrecy to meet outside a hotel I looked up earlier.

I walk up to the shabby hotel, its worn exterior telling tales of years gone by. The paint on the walls is peeling, revealing the weathered bricks beneath. The sign creaks in the wind, its flickering neon lights casting an eerie glow.

As I step inside the dimly lit lobby, the air is heavy with a musty scent. The worn-out carpet beneath my feet leads me to the front desk, where a tired-looking receptionist greets me with a weary smile.

I make my way to the room, the worn-out key in my hand. The hallway is dimly lit, the flickering lights casting eerie shadows along the cracked walls. As I enter the room, a musty smell greets me, mingling with the faint scent of cleaning products. The worn-out furniture bears the weight of countless guests, and the faded wallpaper tells stories of past occupants.

The bed, though not the most comfortable, offers a place to rest my weary head. I gaze out of the window, the view obscured by the grime that has settled on the glass.

In this humble abode, I find solace in the simplicity. It may not be the most luxurious of places, but it offers a refuge from the chaos of the outside world. As I settle in, I embrace the imperfections, knowing that sometimes, you have a rough start that will lead to a better future.

I step outside the old, grimy hotel, the sight of Taylor waiting for me bringing a glimmer of light to the dim surroundings. Her eyes widen as they take in the worn-out facade of the building, disappointment etched on her face.

I can sense her unspoken thoughts, her understanding of our current financial situation.

She knows that we had to settle for this place, despite its less-than-ideal condition.

As we lock eyes, Taylor's disappointment transforms into a compassionate smile. She reaches out and gently squeezes my hand, her touch offering reassurance. Without saying a word, she communicates her understanding and acceptance of our circumstances.

In that moment, I feel a sense of relief wash over me, knowing that I have someone by my side who sees beyond the surface and embraces the reality of our situation.

Later, as we find a quiet corner to sit and rest, Taylor turns to me and speaks softly, her voice filled with empathy. "Filip, I know this isn't ideal, but I understand why we're here. We'll make the best of it, and one day, we'll look back on this as a part of our journey," she says, her words carrying a mix of disappointment and hope.

In her eyes, I see resilience and a determination to make the most of our circumstances. With Taylor by my side, the dilapidated hotel becomes a temporary home, a place where we can find solace in each other's presence amongst the challenges we will face.

I wake up in the musty hotel room, my eyes slowly adjusting to the dim light filtering through the curtains. As I take a deep breath, I notice that the nasty, lingering air from yesterday is gone, replaced by a much nicer scent. Taylor's bed is neatly made, a reminder that she's already up and about. I can't help but feel a twinge of longing for her presence, but I push those thoughts aside, focusing on the day ahead.

As I look at my phone, I see thousands of notifications. Messages from my parents, worried and angry that I ran away. Messages from Darcy, apologising for leaving me. But what I'm intrigued about is that fake account made of me. I search it up and it's gone, no trace of it could be found.

I search up my name on the internet. I scroll and look at all the reports and articles about my disappearance. Police suspect I left with Taylor; they also believe we are close by.

But as I leave and head out to go to work, my mind wanders to my mum. I can't help but wonder how she's feeling, knowing that I'm missing. The thought tugs at my heart, and a wave of sadness washes over me. But I quickly gather my thoughts, reminding myself that I'm working towards a better future with Taylor. I envision the life we can build together, a life where we won't have to worry about being separated or feeling lost.

As I make my way through the hectic streets of London, I come across missing posters of various people. But then, my eyes catch sight of one that sends a chill down my spine - a poster of me and Taylor.

The reality of our disappearance hits me once again, and I can't get my mind of my mum, devastated and alone. Guilt washes over me, and I can't ignore the feeling that I've let her down. She must think that she has let me down too.

A sudden flashback takes hold of my mind, transporting me back to a fateful day last year, the day the tormenting began.

One night, me and my so-called friends thought it would be a blast to go somewhere together. But as I stepped onto the train, they unexpectedly turned around and bolted from the station. I was left standing there, feeling completely abandoned and clueless. With no way to get back home and a dead phone, I was stuck in a bewildering predicament.

It's that memory that caused a chain of events leading to my torment, the night that pushed me to leave now, to escape the life I hated and find a place where I can start anew. The pain of that moment still lingers, but it fuels my determination to create a better life for myself.

Arriving at the shop, I put on a brave face, but inside, I'm on edge. I have to keep a low profile, make sure no one finds out that I'm the missing teenager. It's a constant battle between blending in and keeping my true identity hidden.

Engaging with customers and the manager becomes a challenge as I navigate the fine line between being polite and being distant. Every interaction is a reminder that I can't afford to slip up, that I must remain invisible to those who might recognise me.

As Taylor also tries to keep a low profile, she notices Sophia, her manager, becoming increasingly curious about her sudden change in behaviour. Taylor, wanting to avoid any prying questions, tries to be blunt and dismissive, hoping to deter Sophia's inquiries. However, Sophia, being the kind-hearted person she is, refuses to let Taylor feel distressed and offers her help in looking the part for her job at the designer shop.

Reluctantly, Taylor accepts Sophia's offer and finds herself in awe as Sophia presents her with a one-of-a-kind designer dress. The intricate details and exquisite craftsmanship leave Taylor speechless, but her self-doubt creeps in as she complains about not being skinny enough to wear such a beautiful garment.

In that vulnerable moment, Taylor opens up to Sophia, revealing her past struggles with self-image and her history of starving herself.

Taylor carefully slips into the one-of-a-kind designer dress that Sophia has given her. As she pulls up the zipper, a wave of excitement washes over her. The dress fits her perfectly, hugging her curves in all the right places. Taylor spins around in front of the mirror, admiring how the fabric shimmers under the soft lighting.

A smile spreads across her face as she marvels at the intricate details and the impeccable craftsmanship. The dress makes her feel like a princess, as if she's stepped into a fairytale. The vibrant colours and unique design make her stand out in a crowd, and for the first time in a long while, Taylor feels truly beautiful.

The happiness radiates from within her as she twirls around, the fabric billowing around her like a cloud. She can't help but feel a sense of gratitude towards Sophia for not only providing her with this exquisite dress but also for showing her kindness and understanding.

This moment becomes a symbol of Taylor's personal growth and acceptance of herself. She realises that beauty comes in all shapes and sizes, and that she doesn't need to conform to society's standards to feel truly happy.

As I spot Taylor at her workplace, the designer shop, my jaw drops in amazement. She looks absolutely stunning in that one-of-a-kind dress. I can't help but think, "Wow, Taylor, you look absolutely incredible!" Her beauty captivates me, and I can't take my eyes off her.

Nervously, I suggest a little picnic date, hoping she'll say yes. My heart races as I ask, but to my delight, Taylor agrees with a smile. We walk hand in hand towards a picturesque field, enjoying each other's company along the way. It feels like a dream, like I've found someone who can see who I really am.

In the field, the date unfolds beautifully. We laugh, share stories, and create precious memories. The connection between us is undeniable, and as the sun begins to set, casting a warm glow upon us, I can't help but feel a sense of contentment and happiness.

As the sky darkens, we make our way back to the hotel, our steps in sync. In the quiet moments before falling asleep, I find myself reflecting on my feelings for Taylor. I feel incredibly lucky to have her in my life.

Her presence brings me joy and comfort, and I can't wait to see where our journey takes us. With a grateful heart, I drift off to sleep, knowing that I have found something truly special with Taylor.

Chapter 7
Guilt & Freedom

As I wake up, I find myself alone in the room once again. Taylor has already left for work. I feel a tinge of sadness, but I know it's just another day.

Suddenly, my phone rings, and I hesitate before answering, fearing it might be bad news. To my surprise, it's my manager from the shop. He informs me that they are closing for the day to remodel the store. A wave of relief washes over me, knowing that I can finally have a day to relax.

After hanging up the phone, I feel a sense of happiness. It's a rare opportunity to have some time to myself. However, as the realisation sinks in, I also feel a twinge of loneliness. Spending the day alone can be daunting, but I remind myself that it's a chance to explore my own thoughts and interests.

First, I watch the news to try see if there's any new information about our disappearance and as a matter of fact, there is. Me and Taylor have been declared missing for a few days and the search for us continues. Our parents appear on the screen, talking about how all they care about is our safety. They look lifeless and drained, and my mum begins to speak, directly to me.

"My son, if you are watching this then I apologise for being a horrible mother to you. I just wish I can hug you one more time, and to see that smile on your face I have been missing for years. Remember when we would go out and buy random things to make our house cozy, like candles and blankets. I miss that, I miss you. Please come home and stay safe, I love you Filip." My mum took about 5 minutes getting her words out of her mouth, saying it in a desperate tone. I try and not let the sadness consume me and so I think of something to do. Feeling inspired and determined to create a haven of comfort and warmth, I embark on a day of shopping to surprise Taylor with a cozy apartment makeover.

As I step into the crowded stores, I'm immediately greeted by an array of possibilities. I carefully peruse through the aisles, my eyes scanning for the perfect additions that will transform our humble abode into a sanctuary of tranquility.

With each item I select, I imagine how it will add a touch of charm and coziness to our space. Soft cushions in rich, earthy tones catch my eye, their plushness promising hours of relaxation. I can already picture us sinking into the cushions, enveloped in their comforting embrace.

Next, I find myself drawn to a collection of warm blankets, their textures inviting and comforting. I run my fingers over the soft fabrics, imagining the cozy nights we'll spend wrapped up together, lost in our own little world. That thought brings a smile to my face, a smile I haven't had in a while, fuelling my determination to create the perfect ambiance for us.

As I continue my shopping spree, I stumble upon a display of scented candles, their gentle flickering flames casting a warm glow. I carefully select a variety of fragrances, each one evoking a different mood and ambiance. From the soothing scent of lavender to the invigorating aroma of citrus, I envision the subtle dance of fragrance that will fill our space, transporting us to a realm of serenity and peace.

With my arms full of carefully chosen treasures, I make my way to the checkout counter, anticipation bubbling within me. I can't wait to surprise Taylor with the transformation that awaits her.

As I walk back home, the weight of the shopping bags is nothing compared to the excitement that fills my heart. I unlock the door and step inside our apartment, my eyes gleaming with excitement. It's time to unveil the surprise that I've meticulously crafted. I arrange the cushions on the couch, draping the blankets over the armchair, and strategically placing the candles around the room. The transformation is complete, and I can't help but feel a sense of pride and satisfaction.

But I also can't help but feel a sense of sadness, I wish my mum was here. She'd be proud of me taking responsibility for building a new life.

Now, all that's left is to wait for Taylor's return. I can already imagine the look of surprise and delight on her face when she walks through the door. Our little apartment, once a simple space, has now been infused with warmth, comfort, and love. It's a testament to the effort and care I've put into making our home a place where we can find solace and happiness.

As I sit down on the couch, surrounded by the cozy ambiance I've created, I can't help but feel a sense of anticipation. The minutes tick by slowly, each one filled with excitement and a touch of nervousness. I find myself fidgeting with the edge of a blanket, my mind racing with thoughts of how Taylor will react to the surprise.

Finally, I hear the jingle of keys at the door, and my heart skips a beat. I can hardly contain my excitement as I wait for Taylor to step into our transformed sanctuary. The door swings open, and there she is, her eyes widening in surprise as she takes in the sight before her.

"Filip, what did you do?" she exclaims, a mix of astonishment and delight in her voice. I can't help but grin, feeling a wave of relief wash over me. The hours spent shopping and carefully arranging each item were all worth it in this moment. "It's our little haven." I say, my voice filled with pride. "I wanted to create a space where we can unwind, relax, and feel at peace. A place that reflects the love and warmth we share."

Taylor walks around the room, her fingers gently grazing the soft cushions, her eyes lingering on the flickering candles. She turns to me, her expression filled with gratitude and love. "Thank you, Filip. This is more than I could have ever imagined. It's perfect."

We sink into the plush cushions, wrapping ourselves in the warmth of the blankets. As the gentle glow of the candles dances around us, we find ourselves enveloped in a sense of tranquility and contentment. Our little apartment has truly become a haven, a place where we can escape from the outside world and simply be together.

In that moment, I realise that it's not just the physical items that have transformed our space, but the love and thoughtfulness that went into creating it. It's a reminder that even in the smallest of gestures, we can make a difference in each other's lives.

As we sit there, basking in the cozy atmosphere, I can't help but feel grateful for the opportunity to create this haven for Taylor. And as we embark on this new chapter of our lives, I know that our cozy apartment will always be a reminder of the love and care we have for one another.

As the weeks pass, Taylor and I have settled into our new life, carefully navigating the fine line between staying hidden and enjoying our newfound freedom. We've become experts at being discreet, always mindful of our surroundings and taking precautions to avoid detection. It's a constant dance of caution and excitement, as we savour the thrill of being on the run.

Our daily routine has taken shape, and we've found jobs that bring us joy and a sense of purpose. I work at a small shop, surrounded by the comforting scent of warmness from the customers and the kind heart of my manager. It's a place where I can escape from the reality of our situation, if only for a little while.

Taylor, on the other hand, has found her calling at a designer store. Her creativity blossoms as she sows vibrant fabrics together, each design a reflection of her innermost thoughts and emotions. It's a beautiful sight to behold, and I feel a sense of pride knowing that she has found solace in her work.

In the evenings, we come together, seeking solace in each other's company. We spend our time exploring the city, taking long walks through quiet streets, and discovering hidden gems that only locals know about. We find joy in the simplest of activities, like picnics in the park or watching the sunset from a rooftop.

Yet, within the excitement and newfound freedom, there's a lingering sense of guilt that tugs at our hearts. We can't help but feel remorse for the pain we've caused our families, who are left wondering and worrying about our whereabouts. It's a heavy burden to bear, and it often weighs on our minds during quiet moments.

But in those moments, we remind ourselves of the reasons why we made this choice. We were suffocating in the expectations and pressures of our old lives, yearning for something more. And while our decision may have caused temporary pain, we believe that in the long run, it will lead us to a place of true happiness and fulfilment.

So, as we continue to navigate this uncertain path, we hold onto each other, finding strength in our love and the shared dream of a life filled with freedom and authenticity. And in the midst of our guilt, we find solace in knowing that we are on a journey of self-discovery, where every step forward brings us closer to the people we are meant to be.

Chapter 8
Separation

As I stand behind the counter of the shop, my mind begins to wander, delving into the depths of my existence. The weight of my past trauma bears down upon me, suffocating my sense of self-worth. The memories of being bullied and physically assaulted replay like a relentless film, each scene etching itself deeper into the fabric of my being. I can't help but question why it was me who had to endure such torment, why I became the target of their cruelty.

In the stillness of the shop, surrounded by trinkets and forgotten treasures, I find solace in the solitude. It is here, amidst the hushed whispers of memories, that I contemplate my purpose in life. The scars on my body serve as a constant reminder of the pain I endured, but they also bear witness to my resilience. I am determined to rise above the darkness that has plagued my past, to forge a new path for myself.

With each passing day, I seek refuge in the pages of books, finding solace in the written word. Through literature, I explore the intricacies of the human experience, hoping to make sense of my own. Writing becomes my sanctuary, a realm where I can pour out my emotions and untangle the knots of my existence. It is through the power of language that I strive to reclaim my worth and redefine my place in this vast world.

As I stand here in the shop, surrounded by the remnants of forgotten stories, I am reminded that I am more than the scars that mar my skin. I am a survivor, a seeker of truth and understanding. And though the journey may be arduous, I am determined to find my purpose, to rise above the shadows of my past, and to embrace the beauty of my own existence.

I can't help but feel a glimmer of hope flickering within me. Being declared missing for weeks has granted me an unexpected opportunity to start anew in the city of London. It's as if the universe has granted me a second chance at life, a chance to break free from the shackles of my past and embrace the endless possibilities that lie ahead.

In the serenity of my surroundings, I find comfort in the art of writing. It is through the strokes of my pen that I am able to navigate the labyrinth of trauma, experiences, and emotions that have burdened me for far too long. Each word becomes a stepping stone, guiding me towards healing and self-discovery. Writing serves as a sanctuary, allowing me to express myself authentically and process the depths of my innermost thoughts and feelings.

As I embark on this journey of self-expression, I am filled with a profound sense of liberation. Through my newfound passion for writing, I can finally act like myself, unencumbered by the weight of expectations and judgments. It is within the realm of storytelling that I can truly be free, weaving narratives that reflect my truth and inspire others along the way. Writing has become my anchor, grounding me amidst the chaos and providing a channel for introspection, growth, and transformation.

In this vast city of opportunity, I am determined to carve a path that aligns with my newfound purpose. With each word I write, I am reminded that my life is not defined by the circumstances that led me here, but by the resilience and strength that reside within me. As I embrace this fresh start, I am filled with hope and anticipation, knowing that my journey as a writer holds the power to heal, empower, and shape the narrative of my own life, and help shape other people's lives for the better.

As I sit here, reflecting on our journey, I can't help but feel overwhelmed by the way Taylor and I have grown closer. Running away together has been a leap of faith, but it's also been the catalyst for our deepening connection. Each passing day, I find myself becoming more comfortable in Taylor's presence, and I can sense the same ease in their demeanour.

Our bond is evolving, slowly but surely, and it's a beautiful thing to witness. It's as if the weight of the world has been lifted off our shoulders, and we can finally be ourselves without fear of judgment or scrutiny. In this newfound freedom, our love for each other begins to blossom, like a delicate flower reaching for the sunlight.

There's a profound understanding between us, an unspoken language that transcends words. We've both experienced our fair share of pain and heartache, and it's in each other's arms that we find peace. We hold space for one another's trauma and emotions, offering a safe haven where vulnerability is not only accepted but embraced.

As I pour my thoughts onto paper, Taylor becomes my confidant, my muse. Through my writing, I bare my soul, sharing the depths of my being with them. And in return, Taylor's unwavering support and understanding create a sanctuary where I can explore my vulnerabilities and confront my fears.

Together, we navigate the complexities of our pasts, intertwining our lives and weaving a tapestry of love and resilience. Our journey is marked by moments of tenderness, stolen glances, and whispered promises. We are slowly unraveling the layers that have shielded us, revealing our true selves to one another.

In Taylor, I've found a partner who not only understands my pain but also sees the beauty that lies within it. Our love is a slow-burning fire, growing steadily as we learn to trust and lean on each other. With her by my side, I feel a sense of strength and courage that I never thought possible.

Together, we are rewriting our stories, forging a path that is uniquely ours. And as our love continues to blossom, I am filled with gratitude for the journey we are embarking on, hand in hand, hearts entwined.

As I walk Taylor to her workplace, a high-end designer store, the streets are unusually crowded today. A sense of unease creeps over us, and I can feel my heart rate quicken. Suddenly, I catch a glimpse of a group of people turning their heads towards us, their eyes widening with recognition. Panic sets in as we realise, they've identified us as the missing teenagers.

Without hesitation, we break into a sprint, our feet pounding against the pavement. Fear courses through our veins, fuelling our desperate need to escape. The world around us blurs as our adrenaline-fuelled instincts take over. We navigate through the labyrinth of streets, desperately trying to lose our pursuers.

Every step we take is heavy with anxiety and uncertainty. The weight of the situation bears down on us, amplifying our emotions. Fear and determination mingle in our eyes, as we refuse to let ourselves be caught. We know that our freedom hangs in the balance, and we can't afford to let it slip away.

As we turn corners and dart through alleyways, the sounds of footsteps and shouts echo behind us. The chase intensifies, and our breaths come in ragged gasps. But we push forward, our will to survive overpowering the exhaustion that threatens to consume us.

In this moment, everything else fades away. The only thing that matters is staying one step ahead, outsmarting our pursuers, and preserving the life we've fought so hard to create. We cling to each other, drawing strength from our shared determination and the love that binds us.

Though fear grips our hearts, we refuse to let it define us. We are more than just runaway teenagers; we are dreamers and fighters. And as we run through the streets, our hearts pounding in our chests, we hold onto the hope that one day, we will find a place where we can truly belong.

My heart pounds in my chest as Taylor and I sprint through the chaotic streets of London, the crowd of people hot on our heels. Panic courses through my veins, urging me to run faster, to escape this relentless pursuit. We reach the underground station, our last hope for refuge.

With a surge of adrenaline, we burst through the station doors, desperately searching for an escape route. The sound of our pounding footsteps echoes through the empty corridors as we race towards the platform. The train is there, waiting, its doors invitingly open.

Without a second thought, I leap onto the train, my heart soaring with relief. But as the doors begin to close, my eyes widen in horror. Taylor is still outside, caught in the clutches of our pursuers. I reach out, my fingers grazing the tips of hers, but it's too late. The doors seal shut, and the train pulls away, leaving me feeling like a missing soul in the vastness of the city.

Alone in the empty carriage, the weight of Taylor's absence presses down on me. The silence is suffocating, amplifying the ache in my chest. I'm consumed by a sense of helplessness, my mind racing with thoughts of what might happen to her. The city rushes past, a blur of lights and shadows, as I'm carried further away from her.

I exit the station, as the sun sets over the sprawling city of London, I find myself wandering through its streets, my footsteps echoing against the cold pavement. I am a missing soul, adrift in this vast world, trying to make sense of my existence.

The fading light casts long shadows, mirroring the confusion and uncertainty that swirl within me. Thoughts of Taylor, haunt my every step. I replay our escape in my mind, the moment when we were torn apart, over and over again. The weight of isolation presses upon me, a heavy burden that I struggle to bear.

As I walk, the city seems to grow larger, its towering buildings and long streets stretching out endlessly before me. I feel small and insignificant, a mere speck in this grand tapestry of life. The cacophony of sounds and the vibrant energy of London only serve to accentuate my isolation. I yearn for connection, for the warmth of companionship, but all I find is an emptiness that echoes through my soul.

As I trudge back to my apartment, a heavy cloud of sadness and loneliness envelops me. The weight of losing the only person who truly understood me presses upon my weary shoulders. Each step feels like an eternity as I replay the memories Taylor and I shared over the past few weeks, their bittersweet essence clinging to my heart.

Upon entering my apartment, a flicker of hope ignites within me as I turn on the television. But my heart sinks as the news anchor's voice fills the room, announcing that Taylor has been found after her month-long disappearance. My name is mentioned, labeled as "possibly in London," urging viewers to be on the lookout for me. Fear grips my soul, and I find myself paralysed with worry, my mind racing with thoughts of being discovered.

Recordings of us running away into the underground a shown on screen, of how me and Taylor did not want to be found. Taylor comes onto the screen and talks about why we left. She mentions how me and her have gone through traumatic experiences that she wouldn't like to discuss to the public, then she begins talking to me in a desperate manner like my mum did. "Filip, you need to relocate now. Leave London, go somewhere far, a place where no one can find you. You are the best person I have ever met. Goodbye."

In the dim glow of my bedroom, I lay in bed, consumed by a whirlwind of emotions. The uncertainty of my future looms over me, casting shadows on my restless thoughts. Sleep eludes me as I toss and turn, haunted by the possibility of being found, of losing the freedom I have fought so hard for. But as exhaustion takes its hold, I surrender to the embrace of slumber, hoping for solace and respite in the realm of dreams.

Chapter 9
Relocation

As I wander through the streets, a sense of desolation engulfs me. The towering buildings loom overhead, casting long shadows that mirror the darkness within my soul. Every step feels heavy, as if I'm dragging the weight of the world behind me.

The city's energy only serves to amplify my feelings of isolation. I pass by crowded cafes and markets, but I feel like an outsider, disconnected from the vibrant tapestry of life around me. The laughter and chatter of strangers become distant echoes, further emphasising my solitude.

The rain begins to fall, casting a melancholic haze over the city. Each droplet that lands on my skin feels like a gentle reminder of my own tears. I find myself seeking comfort in the shelter of a nearby bookstore, its shelves lined with countless stories waiting to be discovered.

Lost in the pages of a worn-out novel, I find temporary respite from the turmoil within. The characters become my companions, their journeys intertwining with my own. Through their triumphs and struggles, I find solace in the shared human experience, a reminder that I am not alone in my pain.

As the rain subsides, I emerge from the bookstore, my heart heavy but slightly lighter than before. The city's streets glisten with a newfound clarity, as if the tears of the heavens have washed away some of my sorrow. With renewed determination, I continue my journey, embracing the unknown with a flicker of hope in my eyes.

Though the road ahead may be treacherous and the path uncertain, I know deep within that this journey is not in vain. Through the darkness and despair, I will discover strength I never knew existed. And perhaps, just perhaps, I will find my way back home, not just in the physical sense, but in the depths of my own being.

With each step, I embrace the power of resilience, knowing that even in the midst of chaos, there is a glimmer of light waiting to guide me. And so, I press on, my spirit unyielding, ready to face the challenges that lie ahead, and to find solace in the beauty that can be found even in the darkest of moments.

As I stand on the rain-soaked streets of London, Taylor's idea begins to take shape in my mind. The weight of my past and the uncertainties of the present push me to seek consolation in a place far from prying eyes. A place where I can disappear, even if just for a while, until I find my purpose in life.

The coast beckons me with its promise of tranquility and the vastness of the ocean, stretching out into the horizon. I envision a small seaside town, tucked away from the chaos of the city, where I can find relief in the rhythmic crashing of waves against the shore.

My plan starts to form with each passing moment. I research coastal towns, studying their unique charm and the sense of community they offer. I imagine myself walking along the sandy beaches, feeling the salty breeze on my face, and finding inspiration in the ever-changing tides.

With meticulous detail, I begin to map out my journey. I calculate the distance from London to the coast, considering the logistics of transportation and the best route to remain inconspicuous. I gather my belongings, packing only the essentials, shedding the weight of unnecessary possessions that tie me to the past. The only extra thing I take is the photo Taylor took of us back when we first arrived at London.

In the early morning hours, when the city is still asleep, I quietly slip away, leaving behind the familiar streets that hold memories both bitter and sweet. I board a train, my heart pounding with a mixture of anticipation and uncertainty. The landscape outside the window transforms from urban sprawl to rolling hills, a visual reminder of the change that awaits me.

Arriving at my chosen coastal destination, I take a deep breath, inhaling the salty air that fills my lungs. I find a small cottage nestled among the dunes, its weathered exterior a testament to the passage of time. It becomes my sanctuary, a place where I can rebuild my shattered sense of self.

Days turn into weeks as I immerse myself in the rhythm of the coastal lifestyle. I spend my mornings walking along the shoreline, collecting seashells and letting the sand slip through my fingers. In the afternoons, I sit by the window of a local café, sipping hot tea and losing myself in the pages of books that transport me to distant lands.

As I settle into my new life on the coast, I find ease in the simplicity of my existence. I keep my life basic, relishing in the peace and freedom that surrounds me. The quietude of the seaside town allows me to be discreet, ensuring that I remain hidden from everything and everyone, protecting myself from being found.

In these moments of solitude, my thoughts often drift to Taylor. I can't help but wonder if she's enduring her own personal hell, caught by the citizens of London and turned over to the police as the missing girl. The weight of guilt settles upon me, knowing that she may be suffering because of our choices.

My mind also wanders to my mother, consumed by worry and searching for me. I can only imagine the anguish she must be feeling, not knowing where I am or if I'm safe. It pains me to think of her in such distress, but for now, I must remain hidden.

As I gaze out at the vast expanse of the ocean, the waves crashing against the shore, I find a bittersweet comfort in the peace and quiet. It's a delicate balance between the serenity of this new life and the ache in my heart for the connections I've left behind. But for now, I must stay hidden, keeping my presence a secret, until the time is right to emerge from the shadows and face the consequences of my actions.

Chapter 10
Self-discovery

As I sit here, pen in hand, the salty ocean breeze caresses my face, whispering secrets of the vast expanse before me. Living on the coast has become my sanctuary, a place where I find comfort amidst the crashing waves and endless horizon. It's here that I've found the courage to confront my past, to delve deep into the darkest corners of my soul and bring my story to life.

Writing has become my refuge, a cathartic release for the pain that has haunted me for far too long. Through the strokes of my pen, I weave a tapestry of words, each sentence a stepping stone towards healing. As the ink spills onto the pages, I can feel the weight of my trauma slowly lifting, replaced by a sense of empowerment and acceptance.

The experience of running away, of being missing, has forced me to confront the truth that I had long buried. The torment of bullying and physical assault is no longer something I can ignore or brush aside. It's through the act of writing that I've found the strength to acknowledge the pain and reclaim my own narrative.

But even as I find joy in my newfound freedom, a part of me yearns for home. The memories of my mother's worried face and the ache in her voice echo in my mind. The cliffhanger of my journey remains, hinting at a return to the place where it all began. Will I find the closure I seek? Only time will tell as I continue to navigate the depths of my emotions, one word at a time.

And so, with the crashing waves as my backdrop, I write. I write to heal, to grow, and to share my story with the world. In this coastal haven, I am both the protagonist and the author, crafting a tale of resilience and self-discovery. The journey is far from over, but I am determined to find my way back home, armed with newfound strength and a pen that holds the power to transform my pain into something beautiful.

This is the end of my biographical novel and so thank you for reading. The sole purpose of this book is so I can express myself through the role of a character, to show what would come to be from my imagination and so I can process the traumatic experiences that haunt me. One message I hope you get from reading this book is that no matter what happens, your life will get better. Key things you need to flip your life for the better include dedication and motivation.

Filip Kujawa.

Printed in Great Britain
by Amazon